On Sense and the Sensible

Aristotle's Exploration of Perception and Reality

A Modern Translation

Adapted for the Contemporary Reader

Aristotle

Table of Contents

Table of Contents

Preface - Message to the Reader

Rebuilding the Greatest Library in Human History

Thousands of years ago, the Library of Alexandria was the heart of global knowledge — a sanctuary where the wisdom of every known civilization was gathered and shared freely.

And then, it was lost.

Now, we're rebuilding it — and you are invited to join us.

At the Library of Alexandria, we've set out to make every book available to *every person on Earth* — not just in print, but in every language, every format, and for every reader.

Here's how we do it:

- **Deluxe Print Editions at True Printing Cost** - Order any book as a high-quality paperback, elegant hardcover, or stunning boxset — and only pay what it costs to print. No markups. No middlemen.

- **Unlimited Access to the Greatest Works** - Enjoy thousands of timeless classics — from Plato to Shakespeare to Tolstoy — in beautiful, modern eBook and audiobook editions. Read and listen without limits — for every reader, everywhere.

- **Modern Translations for Every Language & Dialect** - We're reimagining the classics in clear, accessible language — and translating them into every dialect imaginable. Everyone deserves to understand humanity's greatest ideas.

When you visit **LibraryofAlexandria.com**, you're not just accessing books — you're joining a global movement to restore, preserve, and share the wisdom of civilization.

Join us today at LibraryofAlexandria.com

Together, we'll ensure the light of human wisdom never fades again.

With gratitude,
The Modern Library of Alexandria Team

Visit:

www.libraryofalexandria.com

Or scan the code below:

Introduction

Ancient Greece was a civilization famous for its great contributions to philosophy, politics, art, and science. It thrived from the 8th century BCE until the Roman Empire started to decline. Greece's city-states, especially Athens, were the heart of culture and intellectual thought. This was the time when democracy began, impressive buildings like the Parthenon were built, and famous playwrights like Sophocles and Euripides produced their works. The Greeks' curiosity about the world around them laid the foundation for Western philosophy. Thinkers like Socrates, Plato, and later Aristotle, pushed the limits of what people understood about the world.

Greek society was deeply connected to theism, which focused on a large group of gods and goddesses who were believed to control every part of life. But this system did not prevent people from exploring new ideas. In fact, it coexisted with a growing interest in finding logical explanations for nature and human life. Intellectuals would often debate and discuss these ideas in public places like the Agora. Aristotle grew up in this dynamic environment, learning from earlier philosophers, and later challenging and expanding their ideas.

Aristotle's Life

Aristotle was born in 384 BCE in a small town called Stagira, located in northern Greece. His father, Nicomachus, was a doctor for King Amyntas of Macedon, and this allowed Aristotle to be around the Macedonian royal court from a young age. When his parents passed away, Aristotle was sent to Athens at the age of 17 to pursue his education. Athens was the center of intellectual life in Greece, and Aristotle joined Plato's Academy, which was the most respected school of the time. The Academy was a place where students discussed everything from ethics to science. Although Aristotle learned a lot from Plato, he did not always agree with him, especially when it came to metaphysics, which deals with the nature of reality.

After spending almost 20 years at the Academy, Aristotle left Athens around 347 BCE after Plato's death. He traveled around different cities in Greece, continuing to study and learn. In 343 BCE, he was invited to the court of King Philip II of Macedon, where he became the tutor of Philip's son, Alexander, who would later become known as Alexander the Great. Aristotle taught Alexander about philosophy, ethics, politics, and science. Aristotle's influence is visible in Alexander's leadership style, which showed respect for knowledge and strategic thinking.

After teaching Alexander, Aristotle returned to Athens in 335 BCE, where he opened his own school called the Lyceum. Unlike Plato's Academy, the Lyceum focused more on recording knowledge and observing nature. Aristotle and his students performed research, studied animals, and took notes on what they observed. The Lyceum became a major center of learning, and it rivaled Plato's Academy. This is also where Aristotle wrote many of his famous works.

Later in life, after the death of Alexander in 323 BCE, the political climate in Athens became difficult for Aristotle because of his connections to the Macedonian court. Accused of disrespecting the gods, Aristotle decided to leave Athens. He fled to Chalcis, where he passed away in 322 BCE. Even though he had to leave Athens, his legacy lived on through his many writings and the influence of his school, the Lyceum.

Aristotle's Impact on Western Thought

No figure looms larger over the development of Western philosophy and science than Aristotle. A student of Plato and tutor to Alexander the Great, he unified logic, ethics, politics, rhetoric, and metaphysics into a coherent system that shaped intellectual inquiry for centuries. Although his writings reflect the best knowledge of his era, they also reveal a distinctive way of understanding the world—one that balances observation with rigorous logical analysis. Over time, this method has profoundly influenced everything from political theory to modern scientific methodology.

Aristotle approached knowledge as an interconnected whole, seeing each field of study as a vital path toward truth. While many earlier thinkers focused on abstract concepts, he emphasized direct observation of the natural world. By systematically examining and classifying what he saw, Aristotle laid the groundwork for the empirical methods now central to modern science. Although our understanding of nature has evolved, his legacy endures in today's emphasis on evidence-based research.

Logic: The Foundation of Rational Inquiry

Often hailed as the "father of formal logic," Aristotle introduced a system of reasoning that shaped intellectual discourse for over two millennia. In works like the Organon, he analyzed how valid conclusions are drawn from premises and introduced syllogisms—deductive arguments that became standard tools in philosophy, theology, and science. Even contemporary logic, despite its modern mathematical and symbolic advancements, can trace many of its core principles back to Aristotle's pioneering analyses.

Metaphysics: Exploring the Nature of Reality

Aristotle's Metaphysics offered one of the earliest comprehensive explorations of existence at its most fundamental level. There, he described the nature of "being qua being" and introduced the concepts of potentiality and actuality to explain how things change and develop. These ideas deeply influenced medieval scholastics—both Christian and Islamic—who integrated Aristotelian reasoning into their theological frameworks. Today, discussions about consciousness, identity, and free will still reference these Aristotelian notions.

Ethics and the Pursuit of the Good Life

In the Nicomachean Ethics, Aristotle proposed that the ultimate aim of human life is eudaimonia, often translated as "happiness" or "flourishing." He argued that we achieve this through virtue, developed by cultivating good habits guided by reason. His famous Doctrine of the Mean asserts that moral virtue resides between two extremes—for instance, courage lies between recklessness and cowardice. This focus on character formation has profoundly shaped the tradition known as "virtue ethics," influencing modern debates on moral education, personal development, and what it means to live well.

Politics: The Role of the Individual in the City-State

Aristotle's practical approach to ethics naturally extended into political theory. In Politics, he explored various forms of government—monarchy, aristocracy, oligarchy, democracy—and weighed their merits and pitfalls. For Aristotle, a well-ordered polis (city-state) exists not merely for survival or trade but to enable its citizens to live virtuous, fulfilling lives. His conviction that ethics and politics are intertwined remains influential, informing contemporary discussions on citizenship, governance, and justice.

Rhetoric: The Art of Persuasion

In his treatise Rhetoric, Aristotle examined how persuasion works, detailing how arguments must appeal to ethos (credibility), pathos (emotion), and logos (logic). This clear framework for effective communication continues to guide public speakers, legal advocates, and writers. From ancient courtroom orations to modern political campaigns, Aristotelian rhetoric underpins many of the strategies people use to sway audiences and shape public opinion.

Beyond these core subjects, Aristotle made significant contributions to biology, physics, psychology, and aesthetics. In the Poetics, for example, he investigated why humans respond so powerfully to tragic drama, pioneering the concept of catharsis— the emotional release that audiences feel through art. Throughout the medieval period, thinkers like Thomas Aquinas integrated Aristotle's theories into Christian theology, while Islamic philosophers such as Avicenna and Averroes preserved, interpreted, and expanded upon his works.

Across centuries of reinterpretation and debate, Aristotle remains a living voice in contemporary thought. His insistence on systematically gathering evidence and connecting it to logical principles laid the foundation for what we now recognize as the scientific method. His inquiries into human flourishing, civic responsibility, and the nature of argument continue to spark discussion and inspire new research. From personal ethics to societal organization, Aristotle's ideas help us frame enduring questions about how best to live, learn, and understand reality.

In sum, Aristotle stands as a foundational pillar of Western thought. He bridged abstract theorizing and practical inquiry, bequeathing a vision of knowledge that values both reason and experience. From ethics and politics to science and art, his ideas have been woven into countless intellectual traditions. Even today, as we grapple with questions of morality, governance, and truth, we walk in the footsteps of an ancient thinker whose breadth of insight and depth of analysis continue to guide our pursuit of wisdom.

Final Thoughts

By preserving Aristotle's legacy, we protect the intellectual depth and rigor that defined his way of understanding the world. His systematic way of asking questions, his classification of knowledge, and his ethical theories are still relevant today, providing a model for critical thinking across many subjects. This preservation is important not just for philosophy students but for anyone interested in the foundations of human thought and the development of ideas that shape the world we live in.

One of the difficulties in studying Aristotle's work is that his ideas and language are complex. Translating these works into our modern language is a key step in making his profound insights easier for more people to understand. By putting his ideas into today's language, more readers can engage with his thoughts, even if they don't have a background in classical studies. Making Aristotle's work accessible means adapting them to modern ways of thinking without losing their original depth. This helps bridge the gap between ancient and modern readers, making sure Aristotle's work stays relevant.

Section 1

Now that we have fully considered the soul and its different abilities, the next step is to look at animals and all living things to understand which abilities are unique to them and which are shared. What we've already determined about the soul on its own will apply here too. Now, we need to address the remaining aspects that involve both the soul and the body, starting with the most basic ones.

The most important traits of animals, whether shared by all or unique to some, are clearly those of both the soul and body together, like sensation, memory, emotions, desires, and pleasure and pain. These traits can be said to belong to all animals. However, beyond these, there are some traits shared by all living things, while others are unique to certain types of animals. The most important of these traits can be grouped into four pairs: being awake and asleep, youth and old age, breathing in and out, and life and death. We must try to understand these scientifically, figuring out what they are and why they happen.

The philosopher who studies nature must also understand the basics of health and disease because neither of these can exist in things that aren't alive. In fact, we can say that most physical researchers and doctors who study medicine philosophically complete their work with discussions on health, while doctors often base their medical ideas on principles learned from nature.

It's obvious that all the traits listed above belong to both the soul and body working together because they all involve sensation in some way or depend on it. Some are feelings or states related to sensation, others protect and preserve it, and some cause its loss or absence. It's clear from both reasoning and observation that sensation occurs in the soul through the body.

In our work on the soul, we already explained the nature of sensation, how we perceive through it, and why this ability belongs to animals. Sensation must indeed be attributed to all animals because its presence or absence is what separates animals from non-animals.

Now, looking at each sense individually, we can say that touch and taste are necessary for all animals. Touch is essential for the reasons we explained in the work on the soul, and taste is needed for nutrition. It's through taste that animals distinguish between pleasant and unpleasant foods, so they can avoid the bad and go after the good. In general, flavor is a quality of nourishing substances.

The senses that work through external media—smell, hearing, and sight—are found in all animals that can move. For all animals that have these senses, they serve as tools for survival, allowing them to seek food and avoid harmful or dangerous things based on prior sensations. But for animals that also possess intelligence, these senses help them reach higher levels of understanding. They provide information about many different qualities of things, leading to knowledge of truth, both theoretical and practical, in the soul.

Of the last two senses mentioned, sight is more important for basic survival needs, but hearing is more important for developing intelligence. Sight, because all bodies have color, provides information about many different characteristics of things, allowing us to perceive common qualities like shape, size, movement, and number. Hearing, on the other hand, only tells us about the unique qualities of sound and, for a few animals, voice. However, indirectly, hearing contributes more to the growth of intelligence. This is because speech, which teaches us things, is heard. Speech is made up of words, and each word represents a thought. Therefore, among people who are born without either sense, those who are blind are generally more intelligent than those who are deaf and mute.

We've already discussed the unique abilities of each of the senses.

Now, let's consider the nature of the sense organs, or the parts of the body where each sense is naturally found. Many researchers base their ideas on the basic elements that make up everything. But they struggle to match five senses with just four elements, which confuses them about the fifth sense. For example, they believe that the organ of sight is made of fire because when the eye is pressed or moved, it seems like fire flashes from it. This happens most clearly in the dark or when the eyelids are closed, because darkness is produced then too.

But this idea only solves one problem while creating another. Unless we assume that someone can see an object without realizing it, this theory would mean that the eye sees itself. But why doesn't this "flash" happen when the eye is still? The true explanation for this can be found in understanding how smooth things naturally shine in the dark, without giving off light. The black part of the eye, its center, is smooth. The flash only happens when the eye moves quickly because this movement makes one object appear to be two. The speed of the motion makes what is seen and what is seeing seem like two different things. This doesn't happen unless the motion is fast and in the dark. It's in the dark that smooth things, like the heads of certain fish, naturally shine. If the eye moves slowly, the same object can't appear to be two at once. In reality, the eye sees itself in this flash the same way it does when reflected in a mirror.

If the organ for sight really was made of fire, as Empedocles believed, and as it's suggested in the Timaeus, and if sight was caused by light coming from the eye like from a lantern, why can't the eye see in the dark? It's pointless to say, like in the Timaeus, that the visual ray is "quenched" in the dark. What does it mean for light to be "quenched"? Something hot and dry, like burning coals or fire, can be quenched by something cold or wet. But light doesn't seem to have heat or dryness. Or if it does, and it's just so slight we can't notice, we should expect the sun's light to be quenched during rain or in freezing weather. Flames and burning objects can be put out this way, but sunlight is not.

Empedocles sometimes explains vision by light coming from the eye, like in this passage:

"Like someone preparing a lantern

To shine in the stormy night,

Setting clear sides around the fire
To protect it from the wind,

While the fire leaps out and shines

Its constant beams over the threshold."

Here, he explains vision by fire within the eye, but at other times, he says vision comes from things outside the eye.

Democritus, on the other hand, correctly says the eye is made of water. However, he is wrong when he explains sight as just reflecting images like a mirror. The reflection happens because the eye is smooth, and the reflection occurs not in the eye that is seen, but in the one that sees. It's just a case of reflection. But even in his time, there wasn't enough knowledge about how images and reflections form. It's strange that he didn't ask why, if his theory is true, the eye is the only thing that sees, while other reflective surfaces do not.

It's true that the eye is made of water, but it sees not because of that, but because it is translucent, which

17

is a quality shared by both water and air. However, water is easier to contain and condense than air, which is why the eye is made of water. This is proven by actual experience. When eyes decompose, the liquid that comes out is water, and in embryos, this liquid is cold and shiny. In animals with blood, the white part of the eye is oily and fatty to prevent the moisture from freezing. This is why the eye doesn't feel cold; no one feels cold in the area protected by the eyelids. Bloodless animals have eyes protected by a hard scale, which serves the same purpose.

Overall, it doesn't make sense to say the eye sees because something comes out of it. The idea that light from the eye stretches all the way to the stars, or only to a certain point before joining rays from the object, is unreasonable. If this were true, the merging of rays would happen inside the eye itself. But even this is just speculation. What does it mean for light to "merge" with other light? How could the light inside the eye merge with the light outside it, when the membrane around the eye is in between?

We've said before that sight is impossible without light, but whether the medium is air or light, vision happens through that medium.

Therefore, it's easy to understand that the inner part of the eye is made of water, because water is translucent.

Just as vision is impossible without light outside the eye, it's also impossible without light inside the eye. There must be something translucent inside the eye, and since it's not air, it must be water. The soul, or the part of it that perceives, isn't on the surface of the eye but somewhere inside. That's why the inside of the eye must be capable of letting in light. We know this is true from real experiences. When soldiers are wounded in battle by a sword that cuts through the eye's passages, they suddenly feel darkness, as if a lamp went out. This is because the pupil, the translucent part that acts like an inner lamp, is cut off from the soul.

So, if all these facts are correct, it's clear that if we explain the sense organs by matching them with the four elements, we should say the part of the eye involved in vision is made of water, the part involved in hearing is made of air, and the sense of smell is related to fire. (I'm talking about the sense of smell, not the organ itself.) The organ of smell is only potentially what the sense of smell becomes when it is activated by its object. Smell is like a smoky vapor, and smoke comes from fire. This helps explain why the olfactory organ is near the brain, as cold matter has the potential to become hot. The same reasoning applies to the development of the eye. Its structure comes from the brain, which is the wettest and coldest part of the body.

The organ of touch is made of earth, and taste is a specific kind of touch. This explains why both touch and taste are closely connected to the heart, since the heart, being the hottest part of the body, balances the coldness of the brain.

This is how we should understand the characteristics of the sense organs.

We have already discussed the qualities connected to each of the senses, like color, sound, smell, taste, and touch, in On the Soul. There, we talked about their purpose and how they become actual through their respective sense organs. Now, we must explain each of them in more detail—what we mean by color, sound, smell, taste, and touch. Let's start with color.

Each of these can be thought of in two ways: as potential or as actual. In On the Soul, we explained how the actualized version of color or sound is similar to and different from the act of seeing or hearing. The goal of this discussion is to figure out what each sensory quality must be in itself in order for it to be perceived.

We already said in On the Soul that light is the color of the translucent, and this happens when a fiery element is present in a clear medium. When the fiery element is not present, the result is darkness. However, translucence itself isn't something unique to air, water, or any other clear substances; it's a quality that can be found in all bodies to some degree. Translucence doesn't exist by itself but is present within these substances. Since every body with translucence has an outer boundary, translucence must also have one. So, we can say that light is the nature of the translucent when it is not limited by any boundaries. However, when translucence exists within a bounded body, its boundary must be something real. This is where color comes in— color is found at the outer limit of the body, either as part of the body's surface or as the surface itself. This is why the Pythagoreans called the surface of a body its "hue," because hue lies at the boundary of a body. But the boundary isn't a separate thing; we can imagine that the same substance that carries color on the outside also exists inside the body.

Even air and water seem to have color because they are bright, which is similar to having color. But the color of air or the sea is different depending on how far away you are from it. When you get closer, the color changes. In solid objects, the color is fixed unless the surrounding atmosphere changes it. This shows that the thing that allows color to exist is the same in both cases. So, it's the translucence in bodies that causes them to take on color, depending on how much translucence they have. Since color exists at the boundary of the body, it must also exist at the boundary of the translucent part within the body. Therefore, we can define color as the limit of translucence in a solid body. Whether we are talking about translucent things like water or solid things with fixed colors, they all show their colors at their outer surfaces.

The same thing that produces light in air can also be present in the translucence inside solid bodies, or it might not be present, resulting in the absence of light. Just like how air can have light or darkness, solid objects can have the colors white or black.

Now, let's talk about the other colors and go over the different ideas people have come up with to explain how they are created.

1.   It's possible that white and black are mixed together in such tiny amounts that neither one is visible on its own, but the combination of both creates a new color. This new color wouldn't be white or black but something different. This could explain how we get a variety of colors besides white and black. These colors could also be produced by

different ratios of black to white. For example, the ratio could be 3 to 2 or 3 to 4, creating different colors, while other colors might not follow any specific ratio. Some of these colors might be like the notes in music, where certain ratios are more pleasing, such as purple, crimson, and a few others. These colors are rare for the same reason that musical harmonies are few in number. Other colors might come from irregular combinations of black and white. Some colors could be based on precise ratios, while others might be irregular, leading to impure colors due to the way the ratio is arranged. This is one possible explanation for how we get different colors.

2.   Another idea is that black and white appear through each other, creating an effect like what happens when painters layer one color on top of another to make an object look like it's underwater or in a fog. The same thing happens when the sun, which is naturally white, looks red when seen through a fog or smoke. According to this idea, different colors could also arise from this mixing, depending on the ratio of the top color to the bottom color. But it doesn't make sense to say, like some ancient thinkers did, that colors come from objects emitting something. They would still have to explain how sense perception happens through touch, so it's

better to say that perception happens because the object affects the medium between it and the sense organ.

If we accept the idea of colors being side by side, we also have to assume that both the size of the colors and the time they take to appear are so small that we don't notice them. This way, the combination of colors appears as one. But if we follow the idea of one color being on top of another, we don't need to make this assumption. The effect that the top color has on the medium will change depending on whether it is affected by the color underneath it. So, the result will be a color that is neither white nor black. If we can't assume that any size can be invisible, and we have to believe that everything is visible from some distance, then this second idea of colors being layered can also be seen as a valid theory of color mixing.

3.   There is also a third idea, which says that bodies don't just mix by putting their smallest parts side by side, but that their material is fully combined together. We discussed this in the treatise on Mixture. This kind of mixing, where the material is blended together, is the most complete form of mixture. When bodies mix this way, their colors are mixed too, and this is what causes there to be many colors. When bodies mix, the color looks the same from

any distance, unlike when colors are just layered or placed side by side, where the color changes depending on how close you are.

Colors will still be many in number because the materials can combine in many different ratios. Some colors will come from specific ratios of materials, while others will result from irregular amounts. Everything we said about colors being side by side or layered also applies to this kind of mixing.

We will discuss later why colors, tastes, and sounds exist in specific types instead of being infinite in number.

We have now explained what color is and why there are many colors. Before this, in our work On the Soul, we explained the nature of sound and voice. Now, we need to discuss smell and taste. These two are almost the same in how they affect us physically, though they come from different sources. Tastes are easier for us to understand than smells because the sense of smell in humans is weaker than in animals. Among our senses, smell is the least perfect, while our sense of touch is the finest, and taste is a part of touch.

Water, by itself, doesn't have much taste. But since we can't taste without water, we have to think about how water works with taste. Either (a) we can say that water already has tiny, invisible amounts of all different tastes mixed in it, as Empedocles believed; or (b) water is like a base that can develop different tastes from different parts of itself; or (c) water doesn't have any taste on its own, but something else, like heat or the sun, causes it to have taste.

(a) It's easy to see that Empedocles' idea is wrong. When fruits are picked and left in the sun or put near fire, their juices change because of the heat. This shows that the change doesn't come from the water they got from the ground, but from something happening inside the fruit. We also see that juices, when left out, change from sweet to bitter or other tastes over time. Boiling or fermenting these juices can also give them new tastes.

(b) It's also impossible that water is made in a way that different parts of it can produce different tastes, because we see different tastes come from the same water, which is used to nourish them.

(c) The only option left is to think that water changes by receiving some effect from something else. It's clear that water doesn't get its taste just from heat. Water is thinner than any other liquid, even oil. Although oil is thicker and stickier, it's easier to handle than water because water doesn't hold together. Since pure water doesn't become thick when heated, we have to think that something besides heat causes taste. All things with taste have some level of thickness. Heat helps in this process, but it isn't the only cause.

The juices in fruits come from the earth. That's why some of the older philosophers said that water takes on the qualities of the earth it flows through. This is especially clear with salty water from springs, because salt is a type of earth. Also, when liquids are filtered through ashes, they become bitter. Some wells have bitter water, some are acidic, and others have different kinds of tastes.

As we might expect, the plant world has the most variety of tastes. In nature, moist things are affected by their opposite, which is dryness. That's why moist things are affected by fire, which is naturally dry. Heat is the main property of fire, just as dryness is the main property of earth. So fire and earth, by themselves, can't affect each other directly. In fact, no two natural things can affect each other unless there is some kind of opposite quality between them.

Just like people can wash colors or tastes into water, nature does the same thing. It washes the dry and earthy things in moisture and filters it. This happens when heat moves through the dry and earthy parts, giving the water a certain quality. This change, caused by the dry part acting on the moist, makes it possible for us to taste. Taste takes what was just a potential ability to sense and makes it an actual experience. This is similar to how our other senses work, not by learning something new, but by using what we already know.

Tastes belong to food that can nourish us, and this becomes clearer when we realize that neither dry things without moisture nor moist things without dryness can nourish. Only things made from a mix of both can feed animals. The tangible parts of food, like whether it is hot or cold, are what cause animals to grow or decay. Heat or coldness directly causes growth or decay. But it's the taste of food that gives nourishment. All living things are nourished by sweetness, either by itself or mixed with other tastes. We will discuss this more in our work on Generation, but for now, we only need to mention what is necessary for this discussion. Heat causes growth and helps the food become digestible. It pulls in the light things, like sweetness, and rejects the heavy things, like salt and bitterness. The heat inside living things works the same way the heat outside of them does. This is how nourishment comes from sweetness. Other tastes are added to food in the same way we season food with salt or acid to balance out the sweetness. These tastes stop the sweet food from being too rich and light for the stomach.

Just like mixing white and black gives us in-between colors, mixing sweet and bitter gives us in-between tastes. These mixed tastes either have a specific balance or an undefined mixture of the two. Some tastes are mixed in exact amounts, which affects how they stimulate us, while others are mixed in ways that can't be exactly measured. Tastes that are pleasing come from a balance in their mixture.

The sweet taste is rich, and rich can be seen as a kind of sweet. On the other hand, salty is very similar to bitter, since both lack sweetness. Between sweet and bitter are harsh, pungent, astringent, and sour tastes. There are about as many different kinds of tastes as there are colors. We can say there are seven main kinds of each. For example, we could consider gray as a kind of black, or we could group yellow with white, just as rich goes with sweet. The basic colors like crimson, violet, leek-green, and deep blue are between white and black, and all other colors come from mixing these.

Just as black is the absence of white in something transparent, bitter or salty is the absence of sweetness in food. This is why ashes of burned things are bitter, because the sweet moisture has been burned away.

Democritus and other natural philosophers who study sense-perception are wrong because they treat everything we sense as a kind of touch. If that were true, it would mean all of our senses are really just touch, but that doesn't make sense.

They also treat things that all senses can perceive as if only one sense can perceive them. Qualities like size, shape, roughness, and smoothness are things that can be sensed by sight and touch, and this is why we can sometimes make mistakes about them. But when it comes to things that only one sense can perceive, like color or sound, there is no confusion.

They also confuse things that are specific to one sense with things that all senses can perceive, like when Democritus says white and black are just different kinds of rough and smooth. He also says taste comes from atomic shapes. But it's clear that no one sense, or if any, it would be sight, is better at perceiving common qualities. If taste were better at this, it would mean taste could sense shapes better than anything else.

All the things we sense have opposites. For example, white is the opposite of black, and sweet is the opposite of bitter. But no shape is the opposite of another shape. So, which polygon shape that Democritus says is bitter is the opposite of the spherical shape he says is sweet?

Since there are an infinite number of shapes, there should also be an infinite number of tastes. But if that were true, why would we be able to sense some tastes and not others?

This finishes our discussion of taste. The other effects of taste will be talked about more in our study of plants.

•••

Section 2

Our understanding of smells must be similar to how we understand tastes. Just like how dry things with taste affect both air and water but in different ways, the dry things that cause smell affect air and water too, but through different senses. We usually say that both air and water are transparent, but they don't carry smells because they are transparent. Instead, they carry smells because they can wash and absorb the dry substances that create smells.

Smell exists not just in the air but also in water. We know this because fish and shellfish can smell, even though water doesn't have air in it (because any air in water rises to the surface), and these animals don't breathe. So, if we assume that both air and water are moist, then smell is a natural substance made of dry things that have taste, spread out in the moisture, and anything like that would be something we can smell.

We can see that the ability to smell is based on something having taste by comparing things that have smell to things that don't. The basic elements, like fire, air, earth, and water, don't have smells because the dry and moist parts of them don't have taste unless something is added to give them taste. This explains why seawater has a smell—because, unlike pure water, it has both taste and dryness. Salt also has more smell than natron, as we can see from the oil that comes from salt. Natron is more similar to pure earth than salt is. A stone doesn't have a smell because it has no taste, but wood has a smell because it does have taste. Different types of wood that have more water in them smell less than others. If we look at metals, gold has no smell because it has no taste, but bronze and iron do have smells. When the moisture with taste burns out of these metals, the leftover slag has less smell than the metals themselves. Silver and tin smell more than some metals, but less than others, because they contain more water than some but less than others.

Some people think that smell comes from fumid exhalation, which is a mix of earth and air. Heraclitus seemed to believe this when he said that if everything turned into smoke, we would use our noses to sense them. Many people believe that smell comes from some kind of exhalation. Some think it comes from water, others think it comes from smoke, and others believe it comes from either one. Aqueous exhalation is just a form of moisture, but fumid exhalation is a mix of air and earth. When the first type condenses, it turns into water. The second type turns into a specific kind of earth. But it's unlikely that smell comes from either of these. Vaporous exhalation is just water, and since water has no taste, it has no smell. And fumid exhalation can't happen in water, but, as we've already said, creatures in water also have the ability to smell.

Also, the idea that smell comes from exhalation is similar to the idea that it comes from emanations. If the emanation theory isn't correct, then the exhalation theory probably isn't either.

It makes sense that moist things, whether in air or water (since air is also naturally moist), can absorb the effects of dry things that have taste. If the dry things in moist places like air and water create an effect as if they have been washed, then smells must be something like tastes. In fact, this is true in some cases, because we use the same words to describe both smells and tastes. For example, we say that smells and tastes can be pungent, sweet, harsh, astringent, or rich. We can even think of bad smells like we think of bitter tastes. This is why bad smells are unpleasant to breathe in, just like bitter tastes are unpleasant to swallow. So, it's clear that smell in both water and air works in a similar way to taste, which only happens in water. This also explains why cold and freezing make tastes dull and completely get rid of smells, because cold stops the heat that helps create taste.

There are two types of smells. Some writers say that smells can't be divided into types, but this isn't true. We need to explain how these two types can be recognized.

One kind of smell is like tastes. Whether these smells are pleasant or unpleasant depends on other factors. Since tastes are qualities of food, the smells related to them are nice when animals are hungry for the food, but not nice when they are full and don't want the food anymore. These smells aren't pleasant to animals that don't like the food the smell comes from. So, as we said, these smells are pleasant or unpleasant based on the situation, and this is why all animals can sense these smells.

The other kind of smell is the kind that is pleasant by its very nature, like the smell of flowers. These smells don't make animals want food and don't create appetite; in fact, they might even have the opposite effect. As the poet Strattis joked about Euripides: "Don't use perfume to flavor soup." This shows a truth—perfume doesn't belong in food.

People who add perfumes to drinks these days are teaching us to mix different sensations of pleasure, so we start to enjoy a mix of things that should feel separate.

Humans are the only ones who can sense this second type of smell. The first kind, the one connected to taste, can be sensed by all animals. Since the pleasantness of these smells depends on taste, they can be divided into as many types as there are tastes. But we can't say the same for the other type of smell, the one that is pleasant or unpleasant on its own. The reason humans are the only ones who can sense this type of smell is connected to the way our brains are. The human brain is naturally cold, and the blood in it is thin and pure but cools easily (this is why food smells, when cooled by the brain's coldness, can cause unhealthy effects like runny noses). So, these kinds of smells are made for human health. That is their only purpose, and it's clear that they do this job. Food, whether dry or moist, might taste sweet but still be unhealthy, while a pleasant smell is almost always good for our health.

For this reason, the sense of smell works through breathing in, but this only happens in humans and some other animals with blood, like four-legged animals and those that breathe air. When smells, which have heat in them, rise to the brain, they help the health of this part of the body. Smells naturally give warmth. This is why nature uses breathing for two things: first, to help the chest, and second, to let in smells. When an animal breathes in, the smell comes in through the nose, almost like sneaking in through a side entrance.

The second type of smell we talked about is only sensed by humans, and not by all animals. This is because humans have larger, moister brains than any other animals compared to their body size. This is also why humans are the only animals who seem to enjoy the smell of flowers and similar things. The warmth and stimulation caused by these smells match the coldness and moisture in the human brain. For other animals with lungs, nature gave them the ability to sense one of the two types of smell (the one related to food) when they breathe, so they don't need two different organs to sense smell. For these animals, breathing gives them the ability to sense the type of smell they need, just like humans can sense both kinds of smell through breathing.

It's clear that animals that don't breathe can still smell. Fish and insects, for example, have a strong sense of smell for finding their food, even from far away. Bees and small ants, like those called knipes, can smell their food from a distance. Marine animals like the murex and other similar creatures can also smell their food clearly.

It's not always clear which organ they use to smell. This question of how they smell can be tricky if we think that smelling only happens when animals breathe. It's clear that animals that breathe only smell while breathing, but the animals we just talked about don't breathe and still smell things—unless they have some unknown sense. But that's impossible. Any sense that detects smell is a sense of smell, and these animals clearly do smell, though they probably don't do it in the same way as animals that breathe. For animals that breathe, the act of breathing removes something that covers the organ of smell (this explains why they can't smell when they're not breathing). For animals that don't breathe, this covering is never there, just like how some animals have eyelids that block their vision when closed, while animals without eyelids can see all the time.

Based on what we've said, no lower animals avoid things that smell bad unless the bad smell is actually harmful. They can still be harmed by these smells, just like humans can. Humans can get headaches or even die from strong fumes like those from charcoal. Similarly, lower animals are killed by the strong smells of things like sulfur or bitumen. This is why they avoid these smells, not because they dislike them but because they have learned from experience that the smells are dangerous. They don't care about unpleasant smells unless those smells change the taste of their food.

Since we have an odd number of senses, and an odd number always has a middle point, smell is in the middle between touch (which includes taste) and the senses that work through a medium (like sight and hearing). This means that the things we smell are connected to both food (which is a tangible thing) and to things that can be heard or seen. This is why creatures can smell both in air and in water. So, smell belongs to both these worlds, connected to both things we touch and things that are heard or seen. This is why we describe smell as something dry that gets washed in something moist and fluid. That's how we should understand when it makes sense to say that smells have different types.

The idea some Pythagoreans had, that some animals live off smells alone, is incorrect. First, we see that food has to be a mix of things because the bodies it feeds are not simple. This is why waste is produced from food, either inside the body or, like in plants, outside of it. Even water on its own can't be food because something that can nourish must have a solid form. It's even harder to imagine that air could become solid enough to be food. Also, all animals have a place in their bodies to store food, from which the body absorbs it. The organ for smelling is in the head, and smells enter with the breath, going to the lungs. So it's clear that smell, by itself, doesn't give nutrition. But it's also clear that smell is good for health, as we can sense directly and as we've already discussed. Smell is to general health what taste is to nutrition and the body.

This concludes our discussion of the senses and how we perceive them.

One might ask: if every physical object can be divided into smaller and smaller parts forever, can the things we sense, like color, taste, smell, sound, weight, cold, heat, heaviness, lightness, hardness, or softness, also be divided forever? Or is this impossible?

This is a good question because each of these qualities is something we can sense, and they all get their name because they can affect our senses. So, if this is true, our ability to sense them should also be able to divide forever, and every tiny part of a body, no matter how small, should still be something we can sense. For example, it's impossible to see something that is white without it being a certain size.

If the qualities of a body couldn't be divided just like the body itself, we could imagine a body that exists without color, weight, or any other quality like that. This would mean that the body wouldn't be something we can sense at all because those qualities are what we sense. If that were true, then every object we can sense would be made of parts that we can't actually sense. But that can't be the case because objects aren't made of abstract or mathematical parts that don't exist in reality. Also, how would we be able to recognize these hypothetical real things without any qualities? Would we use reason? But reason doesn't deal with physical objects unless it works with our senses.

If this idea were true, it would support the idea of atoms. This could solve the question we started with, but the atom theory is impossible. We've already explained our views on atoms in our work on Movement.

Solving these questions will also explain why the kinds of color, taste, sound, and other qualities are limited. For everything that lies between two extremes has to be limited. Opposites are extremes, and everything we sense has an opposite. For example, in color, white and black are opposites. In taste, sweet and bitter are opposites, and all other senses have opposites as well. Something that is continuous can be divided into an infinite number of unequal parts but only into a limited number of equal parts. Things that are not continuous can only be divided into a certain number of species. Since the things we sense are divided into species, and they are continuous, we have to understand the difference between potential and actual.

This difference explains why we don't see every tiny part of a grain of millet, even though we can see the whole grain. It also explains why we don't notice the sound within a small musical interval, like a quarter-tone, even though we hear the whole song. The extremely small parts of things we sense go unnoticed because they are only potentially, but not actually, visible unless they are separated from the whole. Just like how a foot-length exists potentially within two feet, it only becomes real when it is separated from the whole. But if these tiny parts are separated from the whole, they could disappear into their surroundings, like a drop of flavored liquid dissolving in the sea. Even if that doesn't happen, since the sense-perception itself isn't something that can be sensed by itself or exist separately, we can't sense its tiny objects when they are separated from the whole. But even though these tiny parts are hard to perceive, they are still considered potentially perceptible and will become actually perceptible when they are part of a larger whole.

So, we have shown that some magnitudes and their qualities escape our notice and explained why this happens and how they are still sensed or not sensed. When these tiny parts of things we sense come together in a whole in a way that we can sense them again, not just because they are part of the whole but even when they are separate from it, their qualities, like color, taste, or sound, are limited in number.

One might also ask: do the things we sense, or the movements that come from them (whether we sense them by something being emitted or through some kind of motion), always first reach a middle point between the sense organ and the object, like smells and sounds do? For example, someone who is closer to the source of a smell will notice it before someone farther away, and we hear the sound of a hit after it has already happened. Is this also true for things we see and for light? Empedocles, for instance, says that the light from the sun first reaches the space between us before it reaches the earth or our eyes. This could seem reasonable because anything that moves through space has to travel from one place to another, and that would take time. But since any amount of time can be divided into parts, we would have to assume there is a time when the sun's rays hadn't yet reached us and were still traveling through the space in between.

Now, even if it's true that the act of hearing or seeing happens all at once and doesn't involve a process of becoming, just like how the sound from a hit has already happened before it reaches our ears, we still know that the sound takes time to travel through space. We can prove this because we sometimes hear words from a distance in a distorted way, which shows that sound is moving through space. So, the question is: does the same thing happen with color and light? We don't see something just because there is a general relationship between us and the object, like two things being equal to each other. If that were true, it wouldn't matter how close or far the object is.

It makes sense that this happens with sound and smell because they, like air and water, are continuous, but their movement can be divided into parts. This is why the person closest to the sound or smell perceives the same thing as the person farther away, but the farther person perceives it later.

Some people question this and say it's impossible for two people in different places to hear, see, or smell the same thing. They argue that the same thing can't be divided between them. But the answer is that everyone senses the same original object, like a bell, some incense, or fire. But each person's perception of the object is numerically different, even though it is the same type of thing. This is how many people can see, smell, or hear the same object at the same time. These things, like smells and sounds, are not bodies but are processes or effects of something. If they were bodies, then it wouldn't be possible for multiple people to sense them at once. But they do depend on a body to exist.

However, light is different. Light exists because something is there, not because of movement. In fact, qualitative change, like color, is different from movement in space. When something moves from one place to another, it has to pass through a middle point first (and sound is thought to be the movement of something through space), but we can't say the same about changes in qualities. These kinds of changes can happen all at once. For example, it's possible that water could freeze everywhere at the same time. But even in these cases, if the body being heated or cooled is large, each part of it changes in sequence, with the part next to it changing first. The part that changes first is changed by the source of the change, but the change throughout the whole body doesn't happen all at once. Tasting would be like smelling if we lived in a liquid environment and could sense flavors from a distance before touching the food.

Naturally, the parts of the space between a sense organ and its object don't all get affected at the same time, except in the case of light and sight, for the reasons we just discussed. Light causes us to see.

Another question about sense-perception is this: if it is natural that when two sensory inputs happen at the same time, the stronger one always pushes out the weaker one from our awareness, can we still perceive two things at the same time? This idea explains why people don't notice things in front of them when they are deep in thought, scared, or listening to a loud noise. We should accept this idea and also another one: it is easier to sense something in its pure form than when it is mixed with something else. For example, it is easier to taste wine by itself than when it is mixed with something, or to taste honey in its pure form. The same goes for color or hearing a musical note by itself rather than together with other notes. The reason is that when things are mixed, they tend to cancel out some of each other's characteristics. This happens whenever different things are mixed to form something new.

If the stronger input tends to push out the weaker one, it also means that when they happen together, the stronger one will be less noticeable than it would be by itself. This is because the weaker one blends with it and takes away some of its uniqueness, based on the idea that simple things are always easier to sense clearly.

Now, if two inputs are equally strong but different from each other, you won't be able to sense either one clearly. They will cancel each other out. If this happens, you won't be able to sense either one in its pure form. So, either you won't sense anything at all, or you will sense a mixture of both, which will be different from either one alone. This is what seems to happen when things are mixed, no matter what kind of mixture it is.

Since a mixture is created from some things that happen together, but not from others, and since things that belong to different senses don't mix (for example, you can't mix white and sharp, except in an indirect way, like how harmony is made from high and low notes), it follows that it's impossible to sense two different things at the same time. We have to assume that when two inputs are equal, they cancel each other out because they don't combine into one thing. But if one is stronger, only that one will be sensed clearly.

It's also more likely that the soul would sense two things at the same time when they are from the same sense, like low and high sounds. It's easier for inputs from the same sense to happen at the same time than inputs from two different senses, like sight and hearing. But it's impossible to sense two things at the same time with the same sense unless they are mixed together because once they mix, they become one. And when the object is one, the act of sensing it is also one, and the act of sensing something one is naturally happening all at once. So, when things are mixed, we have to sense them at the same time because we sense them as one. When something is one thing, we sense it with one perception. But when things haven't been mixed, we have two separate perceptions, which means we sense them one after the other, not at the same time. This is because the sense faculty can only have one act of perception at any moment, and since the sense organ is one, it can only focus on one thing at a time. This means that it's not possible to sense two different things at the same time with the same sense.

If it's impossible to sense two different things at the same time with the same sense, it's even less possible to sense things from two different senses, like white and sweet, at the same time. It seems that when the soul perceives something as one, it's because it senses it at the same time with one act of perception. But when it perceives two different things, it recognizes them as two because they are sensed in different ways. For example, the same sense can perceive white and black because they are part of the same type of perception, even though they are different from each other. Another sense, like taste, can perceive sweet and bitter. Both of these senses perceive things in their own ways, but the way they work is similar. For example, taste perceives sweet in the same way sight perceives white. And just like sight perceives black, taste perceives bitter.

If inputs from opposites are themselves opposites, and opposites can't exist together in the same subject, and if opposites like sweet and bitter are perceived by the same sense, then it's impossible to sense them at the same time. It's also impossible to sense things from the same sense that are not opposites but still different from each other. For example, in colors, some are grouped with white, and others with black. The same goes for tastes; some are grouped with sweet, and others with bitter. You can't sense the parts of mixtures at the same time (for example, the octave or the fifth in music, which are ratios of opposites), unless you sense them as one. Only by perceiving them as one can we sense the ratio between the high and low notes as one whole thing.

If things from different senses, like sweet and white, are even more different from each other than things from the same sense, like black and white, it is even less possible to sense them at the same time.

Therefore, if it's impossible to sense things from the same sense at the same time, it's even more impossible to sense things from different senses at the same time.

Some writers on musical harmony say that the sounds we hear together don't actually reach us at the same time but just seem to because the time between them is too small to notice. Is this true or not? Some might take this idea further and say that even when we think we see and hear things at the same time, it's just because the time difference is too small to notice. But this doesn't seem right. It's hard to believe that there could be a moment of time that is too small to notice because it's possible to sense every moment of time. This must be true because it's impossible for a person to be aware of themselves or anything else during continuous time without noticing each moment. If there were a moment of time that couldn't be noticed, then during that time, a person wouldn't be aware of themselves or what they were sensing, and that doesn't make sense.

If there were some amount of time or some object that was too small to sense, then you wouldn't actually be sensing anything during that time or sensing that object. You would only be sensing part of the object during part of the time. For example, if you imagine a line divided into two parts, and that line represents an object and a corresponding amount of time, if you are seeing the whole line, you are seeing it during the whole time. But if part of the time is cut off, you wouldn't be seeing anything during that time. So, you would only be seeing part of the object during part of the time, just like you only see part of the earth when you look at a specific area. But if you weren't seeing anything during one part of the time, then it doesn't make sense to say you saw the whole object during the whole time. This idea leads to the conclusion that you would never see the whole object during the whole time, which is absurd because it would mean you can never fully perceive anything.

Therefore, we have to conclude that all things can be sensed, but their exact size doesn't always appear right away when we sense them. For example, you can see the sun or a rod that is four cubits long from a distance, but you don't immediately know their exact size just by looking at them. Sometimes, something you see might seem like it has no size at all, but nothing you see is actually without size. We've already explained the reason for this. So, it's clear that no part of time is too small to be sensed.

Now, let's return to the original question: is it possible to sense multiple things at the same time? By "at the same time," I mean sensing several things in a single moment, where that moment is continuous and not divided.

First, is it possible to sense different things at the same time but with different parts of the soul? Or should we reject this idea? For example, if we assume the soul perceives one color with one part and another color with a different part, that would mean the soul has multiple parts that are the same in kind because the things it perceives are all colors.

If someone argues that just like we have two eyes, the soul could have something similar, the answer is that our two eyes work together as one organ, and that's why they perceive as one. If the soul is like this, then whatever part of the soul is formed by both would be the true perceiving subject. But if the two parts of the soul remain separate, the comparison with the eyes wouldn't work because the eyes function as one unit.

Furthermore, if the soul needed different parts to sense different things at the same time, each sense would be both one and many, like having different kinds of knowledge. But you can't have perception without the right kind of ability, and you can't have perception without an actual act of sensing.

If the soul doesn't sense multiple things at the same time with different parts, then it's even less likely that it senses things from different senses at the same time. As we've already said, it's more likely that the soul could sense multiple things from the same sense than from different senses.

If the soul uses one part to sense sweet and another part to sense white, then either these two parts form one whole or they don't. But there must be one whole because the general ability to sense is one. What single object does the soul sense when it perceives something that is both white and sweet? There isn't one because no single object is created from combining white and sweet. So, we have to conclude that the soul has one general ability to sense all things, but it uses different organs to sense different kinds of things.

Can we then say that the part of the soul that senses white and sweet is one when it acts as one and different when it acts as separate parts?

Or is the soul's way of perceiving things similar to how things themselves exist? The same thing can be both white and sweet and have many other qualities, while still being one thing. The qualities aren't actually separated in the object, but each quality exists in its own way. In the same way, the soul's ability to sense is one in number but different in kind. It is different in kind for some things and different in species for others. So, we can conclude that the soul can sense multiple things at the same time with one ability, but this ability changes depending on what it is sensing.

We can show that every object of sense has size and that nothing we sense is without size. For example, the distance from which you can't see something isn't a specific point, but the distance from which you can see it is. The same goes for smells, sounds, and all other things we sense without touching. There is a point in the distance where you can't see the object, and a point where you can see it. This point, where the object becomes visible, must be a specific spot. So, if any object were without size, it would have to be both visible and invisible at this point, but that's impossible.

This finishes our discussion of the characteristics of the organs of sense-perception and their objects. Next, we will consider the topics of memory and remembering.

• • •

The End

The End

Thank you for Reading

You've Just Read a Piece of the Greatest Library Ever Rebuilt

Thank you for reading.

This book is one of thousands we're restoring, reimagining, and translating as part of the **Modern Library of Alexandria** — a global movement to preserve and share humanity's most important ideas.

What was once lost to fire and time is now rising again — not just as memory, but as living, breathing knowledge, freely accessible to all.

What You Can Do Next:

- **Keep Reading.**

  Discover more legendary works — in beautiful print, audiobook, or digital form — at LibraryofAlexandria.com.

- **Build Your Own Library.**

  Every title is available as a paperback, hardcover, or collectible boxset — at true printing cost. Craft a personal library worthy of display.

- **Spread the Light.**

  Share this book. Tell others about the movement. Help us translate every timeless work into every language, so no reader is ever left behind.

By finishing this book, you've already taken part in something extraordinary.

Join us at LibraryofAlexandria.com

Together, we're rebuilding the greatest library the world has ever known.

With appreciation,
The Modern Library of Alexandria Team

Visit:

www.libraryofalexandria.com

Or scan the code below:

57